Why Travel Solo?

The 12 Ways Traveling Solo Transforms
Your Personality and Changes Your Life

Michael Pinatton

Published by:

Michael Pinatton and TLF Media

© Copyright 2016 – Michael Pinatton

ISBN-13: 978-1515024033
ISBN-10: 1515024032

Table of Contents

English Translation

Why Travel Solo? was originally published in French as *Pourquoi voyager seul?* released on Amazon on June 12, 2015.

The book was translated into English by Beth Smith, a French to English freelance translator living in Spring, Texas. She specializes in travel and tourism, advertising and marketing, and literary translation.

You can contact Beth by e-mail at BethSmith@itranslatefrench.net or through her website, www.itranslatefrench.net.

Beth's main experiences with solo travel took place during the year she lived and worked in Lyon, France.

The book was then edited by my good friend, Shannon, who lives in Virginia. She made the book better for you.

Ps. In this book, you will find a few links or resources redirecting to French websites. If you wish to read the content, you can use the Google Chrome browser, it will translate it for you.

Why did I write this book?

Traveling solo. What a crazy idea!

For some people, traveling alone means the excitement of a new adventure, but for others, if not most, it means fear and uncertainty.

In 2015, I decided to explore the concept of solo travel; to test it out for myself and to concretely show all of the advantages and benefits of traveling alone.

This book is a manifesto of solo travel. It was written to inspire you and to encourage you to travel on your own.

So, why did I write this book?

People often ask me how I travel alone.

They often tell me I'm brave. Or that I'm crazy.

I don't think I'm either of those things. I just choose the path that makes me happy – the path of personal development and constantly improving my life.

I discovered the initial benefits of solo travel a few years ago, but it was with time and experience that I truly realized its power.

I want to share the knowledge I've gained through my experience, as well as my experiences related to the people I encounter and befriend. I want to show you the other side of solo travel, the one that people don't always see or fully understand.

I want to explain what really happens when you travel alone, describe the changes that take place and the way these changes transform your personality. All too often, people talk about the disadvantages, the problems, and even the fears related to solo travel. It's time to tell another story, to give a different point of view.

I hope that in my own small way, I will help make the idea of solo travel clearer for you, and inspire you to eventually take the plunge yourself.

The "Solo Travel Guide" series

This book, *Why Travel Solo?*, is the first volume in a series of books dedicated to solo travel.

In the other books in the series, I'll explain how to prepare for a solo trip, how to make friends on the road, how to stay safe during your trip and how to finally stop delaying your plans and just go for it.

To find the other books in the series, please visit: http://traverserlafrontiere.com/en/

About the Author

I'm Michael Pinatton. As I'm writing these lines, I'm 28 years old and traveling in South America. And, as you might have guessed, I'm traveling solo.

I'm a French entrepreneur, a globetrotter, and, as of fairly recently, a blogger and podcaster on the French website Traverserlafrontiere.com, whose goal is to show that it's possible to go live in another country.

Ever since my Erasmus[1] in Bratislava, Slovakia in 2008, I've had the travel bug. So, not surprisingly, I've spent over four years traveling roads throughout the world. Every time I set out, I go alone, without knowing anyone where I'm going and often with iffy plans.

So far, I've lived in Slovakia, Canada, Spain, Colombia and the Philippines. I've traveled in most of the countries of Europe and explored parts of the United States, Indonesia, Thailand, Taiwan and Malaysia.

And I'm still alive!

I can assure you that all of these solo trips have literally changed my life. Each time, I am enriched by new cultures, while I discover amazing landscapes and meet extraordinary people. I also learn a lot about myself and,

---

[1] Student exchange program in Europe

occasionally, a few new skills.

The contents of this particular book come from my experiences living abroad the past few years. They stem from my encounters with other solo travelers met over time. Additionally, some information comes from my analyses of interviews that I conducted with various French people living abroad. Finally, many books, blogs and radio shows about travel have significantly helped me in writing this book.

In this book series, I share my knowledge of solo travel, along with the advice and resources you'll need to take the leap and finally live out your dreams.

« Twenty years from now you will be more disappointed by the things that you didn't do than by the ones you did do. So throw off the bowlines. Sail away from the safe harbor. Catch the trade winds in your sails. Explore. Dream. Discover. »

- Mark Twain

Chapter 1: Traveling with Other People

Before discussing the benefits of solo travel, I want to talk about some of the hassles you may experience traveling with a group.

There are many points of contention when people want to travel together:

- Countries, cities, or regions to visit
- Travel dates and length of the trip
- What to do
- Types of lodging
- Travel budget
- What kind of transportation to use
- The rhythm of the trip: slow or fast?
- What to eat
- And many more!

Finding a person who shares the same approach to travel as you do is very difficult. So you often end up with compromises, endless discussions (perhaps even arguments), or your trip is merely directed by what makes the most sense at the time.

This situation is far from ideal, but it's very common

Because we're afraid to travel alone, we decide to compromise some of our plans, some of our desires, even some of our dreams so that everything will go well during a group trip.

Do you want to sleep wherever you find a spot or in a private home, while your companion prefers the comfort of hotels?

Would you rather take an exploratory walk in the hinterlands, but your companion fancies lounging on the beach all afternoon?

Do you want to go out in the evening to check out the nightlife and maybe meet some new people, while your companion would rather spend a quiet night in with a book?

Would you rather set out with a small budget and work things out as you go, whereas your companion prefers an all-inclusive trip with every activity preplanned?

We all have different desires, thus creating the potential of group travel to be riddled with problems and frustrations. This is especially a shame when you're on the other side of the world!

Luckily, the situation isn't all that bad

Don't get me wrong, traveling among friends, as a couple, or with your family can be a great experience! But I recommend that everyone travel solo. Or with somebody. It's far better to travel with someone else than to not travel at all.

You will benefit from the broadening of the mind that one gains from travel.

I traveled several times with friends or as part of a couple and, in general, they were very good experiences. Even if I travel alone most of the time, sometimes I meet up with friends during the trip or come across new travel companions along the way.

I think it's totally possible to find a person who has a similar view of travel and of life. A person who is willing to adapt to situations and/or one that has the same desires as you.

Not necessarily easy, but possible.

For example, a few weeks ago I met a French woman, Jeanne, in a youth hostel. She just spent eight months in South America and did more than 80% of the trip with her best friend. We talked a lot about traveling with a companion versus traveling solo.

She told me clearly that in hindsight, if she were going to do it again, she would still travel with her friend. These two women have complementary personalities and despite any problems that came up, they got along really well during the trip.

Any kind of scenario is possible when you travel. You have to find the one that works for you.

The alternative to solo travel

As you can see, you're free to do what you want, free to travel with whomever you want.

But know that you can also travel on your own.

It's not that scary.

It's not that complicated.

And everyone can do it.

The advantages and benefits of solo travel are huge. Throughout this book, I'll spell out the 12 greatest benefits of solo travel.

Chapter 2: The Freedom to Go Where You Want

The first benefit of traveling solo is the ability to go wherever you want, no matter what the country, region, or city might be. It's up to you to choose your destination.

By traveling alone, you're free to come and go

You can go where you want without having to explain anything to anybody. There won't be anyone to argue against your plans.

You're guided by your instinct and your wishes. If you prefer big cities, you'll spend more time there, but if you favor the calm of an isolated island, no problem, nobody will keep you from going there.

Do you have a sudden urge to leave where you are right now? Take the first bus, taxi or train and get a change of scenery.

Do you feel like going to that festival that everyone has been talking about for days even though it's not on your itinerary? Do it. Find somebody who wants to go there with you and have fun.

Do you want to get away from the throngs of tourists where you are? Ask the locals where you can find a nice neighborhood where tourists don't usually go, and spend the day bargain-hunting over there.

The thing that's really appealing is being able to change your plans quickly and as much as you want. When you're traveling alone, your initial plans change all the time. It's in the DNA of travel and it's what makes things exciting.

When you're in a group, there's more inertia, decisions take more time, and the trip is generally a lot more planned out.

On a personal note

I think I understood the true value of this freedom during my backpacking trip in the Philippines in 2012. I set out with my backpack; I didn't know a soul. And except for a plane ticket to Manila and a flight to the island of Palawan, I didn't really know what I was going to do.

Gradually, as I met people, I was able to decide

which islands interested me, what events I wanted to attend, and so on. With a two-hour flight or a boat trip, I could go wherever I wanted in this magnificent archipelago.

I very often made decisions one day, or moment, at a time. Setting out unfettered allowed me to go wherever the wind took me and wherever I wanted.

For example, I remember that I stayed at White Beach in Puerto Galera for two weeks even though I had only planned to stay for three days for a music festival. I was just so comfortable in my little beachside guesthouse eating fresh fish every day.

On the other hand, I had intended to spend a week or two in Cebu City, with the intention of meeting some people and living in a city for a little while. However, I didn't really like the ambiance, so I only spent two nights there. Afterwards, I took a bus to the Camiguin Islands, where I found myself practically alone with the locals on a spectacular beach for a week.

How will this freedom of movement change you?

You're going to become more independent in the choices that you make. By consulting all available information (on the internet, in books, talking to travelers, asking the locals for advice, etc.), you're going to make informed decisions.

You're going to take more responsibility, because if you make a bad choice of destinations, it will be your fault. You will have to understand why things didn't go well and, most importantly, remember that experience later on.

You're going to understand what you like about a place. You'll experiment and, over the course of time, develop a quick, personal feeling for destinations.

Chapter 3: Move at Your Own Pace

The second benefit of solo travel is traveling at the speed that suits you without having to adapt to other people. It's time to travel at your own pace and to enjoy your trip how you feel like it.

We all have our own travel speed

Some people like to move quickly during their visits, some like to do a maximum number of things in a minimum amount of time. Some like to take the time to appreciate a monument or a natural feature, some like to stay in one place for several weeks to see how the people live.

Some people even decide to stay for months or years because they've fallen in love with the place they're visiting. You meet quite a few of those along the way!

Know that if you're traveling with a companion, you will never really travel at the pace that suits you. There will always be concessions to make.

Some people travel even more slowly. Alizé and Max, whom I interviewed on my podcast[2] like to stay in a single place for several months. They are fans of what people call "slow travel."

On the other side of the coin, there are travelers who like to see things to the max: as many countries, cities, monuments and activities as possible. I'm thinking in particular of Chris Guillebeau,[3] who decided to visit every country in the world before he turned 35. He achieved his goal, by the way. I suggest that you check out his blog or buy one of his books, which are always a great success.

While no traveling speed is particularly better than the next, the best pace is the one that suits you. Your personality, your availability and your objectives.

By traveling solo, you have the freedom to travel at the speed that makes you happy and allows you to enjoy your trip.

---

[2] http://traverserlafrontiere.com/podcast-018-voyager-volontariat/

[3] http://chrisguillebeau.com/

On a personal note

I like to travel slowly, to take the time to see things, talk to people, and get to know the culture. I find travel much more enriching that way.

For example, as I write these lines in March 2015, I'm living in Barranquilla, a city in northern Colombia. It's not a touristy city and there's not a whole lot to do in the area.

I decided to live here for a few months to learn about Colombian culture, improve my Spanish, live among the locals, and work on my various projects.

This way, I won't be able to see all the sights in Colombia, the beaches or the cities. But it doesn't matter. I have my whole life ahead of me for that. By slowing down, I have the impression that I can really feel the pulse of the country and that I can understand its issues more easily.

Undoubtedly, if I had a travel companion, he or she wouldn't have liked this slow pace.

How will choosing your pace change you?

Traveling at the speed you like will make you happier, plain and simple. You're taking your life in your hands, and it's unfolding based on your objectives or simply on your feelings at the moment.

By now I hope you can see that your pace doesn't have to be dictated by someone else and that it's more gratifying to do as you wish. However, it can make the return to the daily grind, where our choice of schedules and places is more restricted, fairly difficult.

In any case, take advantage of your freedom while you're on the road.

Chapter 4: Spend Time with Whomever You Want

The third benefit of traveling solo is being able to decide who you're going to spend time with.

I love meeting new people when I travel. It's one of the main reasons I go away. Meeting locals or other travelers is the best way, in my opinion, for you to learn new things about the world around you.

When we travel in a group, we have a tendency to keep to ourselves, in the heart of the group, and don't necessarily open up to other people. There's an understandable herd mentality that reassures us.

Missed opportunities

The problem is, by staying with your travel companions, you miss out on a lot of amazing opportunities to meet different people. These occasions are there during every moment of a trip.

Think about your last group trip, whatever it was. How many strangers did you talk to for longer than five minutes each day?

The number probably isn't huge, and that's normal. By traveling alone, you can multiply this number by 10. Those are all extra opportunities for you.

We all have different affinities and different types of personalities we like to spend time with. Your travel companions might prefer to meet people from home or other tourists, whereas you would rather meet locals who have a culture that's completely different than your own.

What can you do? It's never easy and, once again, it's a question of compromise.

For me, one of the major strengths of solo travel is that it leads you toward other people. You can find out about their stories, their worlds, and their ways of life. You'll digest a ton of new things.

And if you don't like somebody, all you have to do is say, "Good-bye." You don't have to put up with people or get worked up for nothing.

It's also a good way to be alone

When I say you make a choice to spend time with

who you want, that also means spending time alone.

If there's a time when you just feel like being by yourself, nobody will bother you by saying that you're "going out on your own" or that you're "ruining the mood."

Introvert or extrovert, I think we can all benefit from some time to ourselves.

On a personal note

I'm fairly introverted by nature and really enjoy my time alone. I can work, read, play sports, learn new things, meditate, and the list goes on.

That's one of the reasons I travel solo. Admittedly, being with someone 24/7 is kind of complicated with my personality.

Yet, on the other hand, I love spending time with new people.

What I want is to have the choice not to have to put up with someone I spend my time with. I want to spend more quality time with people I like and eliminate (so to speak) the people in my life who give off negative vibes.

How is choosing people going to change you?

You're going to decide who you want to spend time with, which is invaluable.

If you've decided to learn a new language, spend time with someone who speaks it so you can practice and improve.

If you've decided to be a little more adventurous or athletic, find a local or an experienced traveler who will teach you things or take you on new adventures.

Finally, your ability to be picky about the people you choose will help you understand how people influence your behavior as well as what kind of people you want to spend more time with. That's a lesson that will serve you well even after your trip.

Chapter 5: Do What You Really Want to Do

The fourth benefit of solo travel lets you live the life you want and do what you love.

After the freedom to go where you want, at the pace that you want, and with whom you want, let's top it off with doing what you want.

Do things that you like, eat in your favorite places, sleep when you want, party if you feel like it, or do nothing at all.

That really speaks to me. It probably speaks to you, too!

Group activities

Every time you travel in a group, you can be sure that each person will want to do different things. Guaranteed! We all have different wishes and passions. It's only natural.

Let me give you some examples:

- You're the sports vacation type, but your friends are the "vegging out" vacation type.

- You're a party animal, but your friends are early risers.

- You'd rather eat local food, but your friends prefer big fast-food chains.

- You prefer spending time out in nature, but your friends like to see every monument in the city.

- You're very gregarious and like to talk to a lot of people, but your friends would rather keep to themselves within the group and aren't really curious.

Of course, you can do your preferred activities on your own, but it often goes against the "group dynamic" to do things alone. That's going to lead to useless discussions, even arguments.

This is why there was "free time" at summer camp. But we're not at camp now, are we?

How do you avoid all of that?

You could have guessed. It's in the title of the book: travel solo. Then you'll have the time to do exactly what you want.

The advantage of solo travel is being able to meet people who want to do the exact same thing as you, possibly even a new friend.

Here's a common example of what happens in youth hostels:

It's Friday night, you arrive in a new city and you're alone. But you'd like to go out and have a few drinks in a bar.

If you talk to the other travelers around you, chances are very high that you'll meet another person (or a group) who wants to do exactly the same thing you do!

In just a few hours, you'll have accomplished two things: had fun and met someone new.

On a personal note

I remember one time at a Couchsurfing[4] meeting in the Philippines, I met a woman who loved scuba diving.

It was a sport I'd always wanted to try, even more so since I was in a country considered a "scuba diving paradise." A few days after talking to this woman, I left

[4] If you're not familiar with it, Couchsurfing is a hospitality exchange and social networking website. The site provides a platform for members to either host travelers or for travelers to "surf" on couches by staying as a guest in a host's home. Check it out: https://www.couchsurfing.com/

with her for a trial dive and I was quickly won over.

Since then, I've gotten my PADI certification and made dozens of dives in Asia.

Thanks to that experience, I've had some incredible moments underwater and learned a sport I truly enjoy. I even swam with sharks in Ecuador!

How this freedom of activities is going to change you

I think that to be happy, we have to do things that make us happy. Regularly. No matter what they are.

By making the choice to do what you want and not deal with other people's wishes, you are – quite simply – going to be happier. Find out what things help you move forward and develop in life.

One big benefit of travel is being able to experience a lot of new things that you couldn't necessarily do at home, either because they don't exist or are very expensive where you are. Diving is one of these activities, but other extreme sports or country-specific sports, such as Thai boxing, are often more accessible abroad.

Chapter 6: Become More Independent

The fifth benefit of solo travel is becoming more self-reliant in your life.

It goes without saying that when we were born, we were dependent. We were unable to meet our own needs.

One of our goals in life is to be able to evolve and manage on our own. It's a process that takes time, for some more than others, depending on each person's life and environment.

Travel broadens the mind

I can confirm that traveling alone is one of the best ways to increase your self-reliance and independence. You're going to find yourself alone in a strange place and need to survive on your own!

Finding your way in a new city, searching for a place

to stay, feeding yourself three times a day, deciding how to spend your days and what direction to take with your trip. There are so many decisions that you have to make alone, which will force you to handle things yourself.

Are you lost? You're going to ask someone for directions.

Are you bored? You'll find something to do.

Are people suggesting several different activities? You'll have to make a choice.

When you travel solo, you're constantly forced to make choices (some more important than others).

The daily-routine "autopilot mode" that you might use at home is long gone. You have to fend for yourself, which is how you evolve.

You have to become more responsible because it's essential to take care of your organization, safety, and budget, and none of that is innate. You learn with experience.

On a personal note

I remember when I set out to study alone in Slovakia for a semester when I was 22.

I had never lived outside the family cocoon. My culinary knowledge was practically non-existent. I had always lived in a familiar environment and had never been alone in the unknown.

As I explain in one of my blog posts,[5] I learned so much during that experience, particularly how to be independent and how to handle my freedom. The thing I regret most is that I didn't go away earlier – at 18!

Get your independence on the right track

Being self-reliant and independent are qualities that help you for your whole life; no matter where you are or what you are doing. Your personality is going to change and you will see that you don't need anybody to achieve your dreams.

To illustrate this idea, I really like this quote from Jinna Yang:[6]

"Well stop waiting around for someone else to make it happen, and make it happen for yourself. When you take control and travel solo, you're forced to rely on yourself."

In short, take control of your life!

---

[5] http://traverserlafrontiere.com/erasmus-bratislava/

[6] http://greaseandglamour.com/

Chapter 7: Find Yourself. Be Yourself.

The sixth benefit of solo travel is being able to discover yourself without all of the "noise" that surrounds us in daily life.

You're alone, far from everyone you know, in a strange place. Maybe it's time to be yourself.

Yes, you, without the superficiality created by our western society, without the preconceptions that other people have about you, without the obligations you've made for yourself, without the technologies that surround you.

Just you. Your body. Your mind.

Traveling solo also means discovering yourself

We study, we work, we have leisure activities, we go out, we have families, and we are rarely alone. Daily routine makes us used to repeating our actions again and again without really knowing why we do them.

By traveling alone, you're going to explore and discover all of the facets of your personality that are rarely used during the course of the daily grind.

You'll explore how your body reacts to different stimuli, how your mind works in a new environment, and how you express yourself with strangers.

When you're traveling, your emotions are intensified. That's when you find out who you really are.

Setting out on your own doesn't mean feeling lonely for the entire trip (see Chapter 11 about meeting people), but it allows you to be alone when you feel like it. Whether it's in a hotel room, in a temple, in the middle of a forest, underwater, at the top of a mountain, or under the stars during a night of camping, you'll find the time to think deeply about the meaning you want to give your life.

Traveling alone lets you reflect on yourself. It gives you time to really think about who you are and what you want to do. It lets you take the necessary step back.

The real you

When you travel solo, you finally have the chance to

be yourself. None of your family or friends can judge you and you're free to do what you want.

Is your creative spirit hindered by living at 100 miles per hour in the city? Finally take the time to explore wide open spaces, new scenery, new sensations, in order to express yourself.

Do you feel like you hold yourself back in your social life? When you're abroad, let yourself go! Find out your limits and do what you thought was impossible to do back home (while respecting others and local customs, of course).

Finding yourself alone in a foreign country puts you in the role of a stranger. So it will be that much easier to be natural and to introduce yourself as you are, the real you.

On a personal note

I learned a lot about myself during my solo travels.

I learned that I liked to travel alone. I like the freedom that that kind of trip provides.

I also learned that I couldn't please everyone. I learned patience. I learned to smile. I learned humility. I also learned that it was possible to do anything and to learn anything in this world. The limits on our abilities are created in our own minds.

I think that learning about ourselves increases tenfold when we travel alone.

Self-discovery

Traveling solo also means taking an internal trip to discover yourself, your personality, the purpose that drives your life, your qualities, your relationships with others, your faults, and your way of life.

And you know what? If you want to use your imagination, why not invent a new life for yourself? Make up a life story – no one will know, and it could be fun!

Take advantage of this solo trip to finally be yourself or to find out who you really are.

Chapter 8: Amélie's Story

Traveling solo may seem terrifying. Maybe you're still hesitating to take the plunge. What could be better than stories from people who have already done it before you?

That's why I'm offering you two exclusive interviews. The first is Amélie. She's a backpacker who prefers long-term travel. She's only 29 and has already crossed several continents in the past few years.

You can read more about her adventures on her blog (in French): http://mamaisonsurledos.com/

1 — When did you set out alone and for how long?

My first real solo trip was when I went to Australia in 2009 with a PVT (in English, it's WHV – Working Holiday Visa). I had traveled in Europe and lived in England, but this trip to Australia was different. I set out all alone to discover the unknown on the other side of the world, telling myself that I was going to make a place for myself. I didn't have any particular plan, I just wanted to completely change my life.

So I landed in Melbourne where I found a little job as a waitress and the best house share in the world. I lived there for eight carefree months, traveled all over the country, and met some wonderful people who are still close friends today.

That first solo trip gave me everything I needed and I returned to France much happier.

2 — What continents/countries have you visited?

Australia, of course! Then, I traveled around Asia, where I fell in love with Cambodia and the Philippines. I roamed around Europe, checked out the New York vibe, then moved on to Argentina. South America is vibrant and exciting. I plan to go back to live there, I love it so much.

Despite its flaws, Argentina is very endearing. And Latinos are the best! I made some wonderful friendships there, which, among other things, allowed me to visit Venezuela to meet my friends' families. It was a real eye-opener for me, and if you ask me about Venezuela today, be prepared for me to go on about it for at least 20 minutes. Haha! I took the opportunity to visit the neighboring countries: Paraguay, Uruguay, and Brazil.

It's funny because people often ask me how many countries I've visited and I can't even tell them. Honestly, I'm happy not counting them!

It's a choice. I'm not running a race. Instead, I savor the pleasure of taking my time. I love spending several months in a country to get to know its people, integrate into a new environment, and create a new routine. I come out of it a better person every time!

I think you have to spend at least six months in a country to start to know it.

3 — Why did you decide to travel solo?

Very simply, because I wasn't very happy in France.

I had a beautiful apartment, a good job, I was buying a lot of things, and yet, something was missing. I had a full social life, but something was still missing.

When I thought about building a career, buying an apartment, and moving in, it didn't make me dream. On the other hand, when I thought about taking a road trip, exploring Asian temples and swimming in crystal clear waters, my eyes lit up!

So, I got moving and I tried my luck!

I wanted to travel alone to put myself in a difficult position. It seems a bit masochistic when I say it like that, but I know I was focusing on things that weren't important. By starting from scratch somewhere else, I wanted my problems to be more basic: finding a way to earn money, finding somewhere to stay and making friends. I told myself that I wouldn't have time to pollute my mind with trivial concerns during this time. And it worked!

That allowed me to be calmer, to gain confidence in myself, to know what my values were and what I should concentrate on.

In the end, everything we do in life is to feel emotions. We work to earn money and to feel useful, we earn money to buy things and to feel sexy, we love to feel loved.

I decided to travel to feel alive and to constantly challenge myself!

4 — What's your best memory of the trip?

That's not an easy question to answer! There are so many.

I'm torn between trekking on the glaciers in

Patagonia and my road trip in a van in Australia.[7]

These two experiences let me taste complete freedom. I felt like I had the soul of an explorer and I saw amazing scenery!

5 — What was your worst experience?

Honestly, I didn't have any huge problems when I was traveling.

My biggest scare was when I was stopped at the airport in Venezuela and was treated to a search and a never-ending interrogation in customs. The way it all happened, I was in a cold sweat and I really believed that someone had hidden drugs in my backpack. But, oh well, in the end, it all turned out ok!

6 — Can you tell us a story that illustrates what "solo travel" means to you?

Paradoxically, for me, solo travel is best illustrated with all the wonderful encounters you have on the road.

I set out alone, yet I was always surrounded by

---

[7] Her articles about Patagonia and Australia:
http://mamaisonsurledos.com/ ameriques/trekking-sur-glacier-perito-moreno-patagonie/
http://mamaisonsurledos.com/ oceanie/road-trip-en-australie-mode-demploi/

incredible people! By traveling solo, I was independent and I gave myself the chance to meet people who were different than my usual circle of friends. I learned to be more tolerant and open-minded.

For example, while traveling in Buenos Aires I met Frayimna, an eccentric, little Venezuelan woman with a contagious laugh. We got along really well, so she suggested that I come live with her in her house share. Four months later, I settled in Argentina and decided to live there for a year! A few months later, I celebrated Christmas with her family and I danced the merengue with her father in the town square of a village in the heart of Venezuela.

You see how far a chance encounter can take you!

7 — What was your assessment of that first solo trip?

Super positive! I was different when I returned to France.

So different that I had to hit the road again! A year later, I left to live in South America, where, among other things, I met my boyfriend, who happens to be Australian! Everything is connected and nothing happens by chance! I really think we forge our own path with the choices we make every day! So now I live in Australia!

8 — In your opinion, why should everyone try traveling solo?

Very simply, to see what goes on elsewhere and to learn to put things into perspective. We have a tendency to complain, especially us, with our French stubbornness. We always see what we don't have instead of being grateful for what we do have!

Traveling puts us in uncomfortable situations where we have to learn to get by. Then, we start to fully appreciate little pleasures, give a lot of importance to the people around us, and stop focusing on our own interests.

Besides that, it would do a lot of people good to become aware of the environmental challenges we're facing and to change their consumer habits.

9 — With your experience, what advice would you give to "Pre-Travel Amélie"?

Go for it! The road is great!

Believe in yourself, dream big, and see the positive in each person and each experience!

Thank you, Amélie, for sharing your story.

Chapter 9: Adapt to Anything

The seventh benefit of solo travel is improving your ability to adapt to any situation.

When you're traveling, you run into other cultures, other ways of thinking, and environments that are much different than at home.

Whether it's though culture shock (food), an emotional shock (poverty), or a physical shock (climate), you're seriously put to the test during your solo trip. The good news is, these tests make you stronger and allow you to build a stronger character.

Adapting in a foreign country

You absolutely have to adapt to your host country, rather than vice-versa.

You often see tourists or travelers who try to import their cultures and their customs when they travel and it usually doesn't work. That's why the French have such a reputation for being complainers in other countries.

Not respecting local rules, not respecting the customs, and not respecting the locals are attitudes you should get rid of. They can ruin your trip.

Two examples

For example, in the United States traffic laws are very strict, as are rules for pedestrian/car interactions. Don't even think of crossing the street when the light is green, don't drive faster than the speed limit, don't park wherever you want, and so on. The fines are a major deterrent!

On the other hand, there are Asian countries (such as Indonesia, Thailand, and India) where traffic laws are of little importance, but respecting other people and respecting religion is very important. If you try to go into a temple wearing indecent clothing, or try to settle a conflict using strong-arm tactics (like raising your voice or coming to blows), you won't get anywhere. Quite the contrary.

When you're in contact with different populations, different cultures, different environments, and different languages, you're going to learn to adapt to the context.

On a personal note

The first time I set foot in Southeast Asia, I suffocated! When I arrived in Kuala Lumpur in Malaysia, the climate was unbearable! It was very hot, very humid, I was sweating, I felt ill at ease, and I was honestly asking myself what I was doing there.

Three days later, I landed in the Philippines and, yet again, felt oppressed in Manila, in that huge, tropical city that was polluted, noisy, had people everywhere, and was very poor.

Little by little I got used to it, and now these sudden changes no longer bother me. When I went to Indonesia and returned to the Philippines in 2014, the difference in climate hardly mattered to me at all.

Now I adapt much more easily to the countries I visit.

How adaptability changes you

Change implies adaptation. For centuries, for millennia, the environment has changed and man has adapted. It's in our nature.

Everything changes quickly when you're traveling alone and you don't have a travel partner to cling to. You have to adapt and evolve.

That can be complicated at the beginning, but you're naturally designed to adapt. After a few adjustments, you will be a lot more at ease.

It's an ability that will serve you well in everyday life.

Let's take the example of a new job, a move, or a personal situation that's changing. You lived through a lot worse during your solo trip! You adapt more quickly.

The more you travel, the greater your ability to adapt will become.

Chapter 10: Learn to Like Challenges

The eighth benefit of solo travel is facing the challenges of daily life with ease and being able to outdo yourself.

Traveling alone is a challenge in and of itself! You already knew that.

During your trip, each day could turn out to be a real challenge. You're going to constantly go outside your comfort zone, learn new things, and become comfortable with the unknown.

Types of challenges

When you travel, you're faced with new challenges that likely never would have come up in your everyday life. It's the excitement and adrenaline everyone is (or should be) looking for in life!

These are some of the challenges you may face when traveling alone:

- Learning basic words in a foreign language so you can communicate
- Trying to take public transportation (bus, subway, etc.)
- Talking to a stranger to learn his story
- Setting off for a day of discovery in a new neighborhood or city with neither a map nor a phone
- Hitchhiking to get around
- Trying unfamiliar food
- Sleeping at a stranger's place through Couchsurfing

Although terrifying in the beginning, these challenges become child's play little by little over time. They allow us to gain confidence in ourselves, to be less shy, and to learn a lot about ourselves.

Besides these everyday challenges, we tend to do more activities that are unfamiliar or riskier than we would at home. It's often less expensive, and taking risks is inherent in solo travel.

Not to mention that we generally have much more time to do these things!

On a personal note

As I'm writing this book (March 2015), I'm in Colombia, and last week I acted as a judge for French contestants in a singing contest. Then, one of the organizers asked me if I'd like to be on a radio show that broadcasts live in all of Latin America.

I had never done anything like that in my life, but I saw it as a challenge and I went for it! Oh, and it was in Spanish.

I probably wasn't very good, but it was an interesting experience, and I had fun with the radio host.

Another example that comes to mind is when I tried paragliding for the first time when I was in Malang, Indonesia. Adrenaline guaranteed!

How will these challenges transform you?

Heading for the unknown, experimenting, and doing things you didn't think you could do: these are the joys of solo travel.

Your personality is inevitably going to change. Furthermore, you'll no longer see those things as risks.

When you return home, talking to that stranger, going to that party alone, achieving an athletic feat, or any other challenge will no longer be a big deal.

Throughout the course of your travels (even more so if you travel solo), challenges will be more easily met thanks to your experience. You will feel more confident to face whatever happens in life.

Chapter 11: Meet More People

The ninth benefit of solo travel is meeting a lot of people along the way and expanding your social circle exponentially.

Whether they are locals, travelers, or expatriates, during your trip you'll have a lot of opportunities to meet new people.

When we're with a group, we have a tendency to stay within the group. When we're traveling alone, the opposite happens. We're much more open to other people.

You're rarely alone when you travel solo

That's one of the big misconceptions when you talk about traveling solo. A lot of people think that you're going to stay alone in your corner, bored, and you're not going to talk to anybody.

Nothing could be further from the truth. Even for the shyest of people!

When you're traveling alone, two things happen:
- You're dying to talk to people (if not, you stay alone)
- You're far more approachable (because you're alone)

The combination of these two factors means that we're more open and that we approach people more easily.

If you ask anyone who has decided to travel alone whether it's easy to meet people, most of them will say yes. These encounters are some of the best travel memories.

Meeting people on the road will make your trip much richer. Friend for one evening, travel companion, travel romance, welcoming host, or friend for life. No matter what types of encounters you have, they will make you better and help you expand your social network.

I think the three easiest ways to meet people while traveling are:

- Staying in a youth hostel and hitting it off with other travelers

- Using Couchsurfing to stay in someone's home or participate in an event
- Asking the locals questions about their towns/neighborhoods

On a personal note

I no longer count the friendly encounters I have while traveling. There are many of them; some are very short, others very long, but all are rewarding.

For example, in March 2014, I set off for three weeks' vacation in the Philippines. The goal was to rest, get away from the Parisian grey skies, see some friends, and enjoy tropical island life.

Near the end of my stay, I decided to spend four days on the island of Boracay. I hesitated a good bit before going because it's a very touristy place and fairly expensive. I decided to go for it anyway, with the idea of partying, enjoying its magnificent beach, and seeing a friend I had met two years earlier.

My friend didn't have a lot of time for me because she worked a lot. Not discouraged in the least, I set out to find some new friends to have fun with. That very night, there was a pub crawl – a kind of party where travelers pay $20 to go to several bars/clubs with free drinks and a guaranteed atmosphere.

I arrived at the meeting point for the crawl decked out with a yellow t-shirt and a shot glass, ready for the night! It's usually really easy to talk to people at this kind of event. It's enough to say, "Hi, where are you from?" to get the conversation started.

Anyway, I met and talked to so many people that night, but I had an especially good rapport with Alejandra, a Colombian woman. We got along well and I nearly spent my entire stay on the island with her. I was able to practice my Spanish, which was very rusty at the time.

When I returned to France, I didn't expect to see her any time soon. She lived in Belgium and was traveling in Asia and South America. When I decided to buy my plane ticket for Colombia in October 2014, I got in touch with Alejandra to ask her for advice about her country.

Imagine my surprise when she told me she had gone back to live in Bogota! So, once I arrived, she helped me get started and played tour guide around the city. There's no doubt I'll see her again one day.

This type of situation occurred several times during each of my trips. I meet people in every corner of the world, we cross paths again, and, in the end, I have tons of new friends!

What all of these encounters change for you

First of all, more encounters mean more opportunities, whether it's during your trip, your professional life, or your love life. All of these meetings allow you to do things you wouldn't have had a chance to do in another context.

The friends you're going to make when traveling alone will be different than the ones you have at home. Different personalities, different nationalities, and different outlooks on life. All of which will help you expand your horizons and learn about the world, others, and, more importantly, yourself.

By reaching out to others and meeting new people, you'll become less shy and more confident. Moreover, you'll be more at ease in social situations and you'll have a better grasp on people and their reactions.

What are you waiting for? Go make new friends!

Chapter 12: Develop Your Open-Mindedness

The tenth benefit of solo travel is becoming someone who is more tolerant and much more open-minded.

This notion of open-mindedness is linked to travel in general, but I think that it's stronger when we decide to travel solo. In that situation, we're influenced by the countries, cultures, and situations we find ourselves in.

Why does that open your mind?

By setting out to travel on your own, you find yourself in a new environment, which may or may not be different than home depending on your destination. Inevitably, there will be a culture clash, things that you find strange, interesting, disgusting, exciting, and/or boring. The more the country differs from your culture, the greater the shock will be.

By traveling alone, you can:

- Learn from other cultures
- Learn from other values or morals
- Learn from other ways of life
- Observe other ways of thinking

Of course, you probably won't agree with everything you're going to see or experience, and that's normal. Simply observing these new things will help you to have a better understanding of the world around us.

For example, I've had these thoughts since the beginning of my trip in November 2014:

- Sometimes we wonder why an entire family (grandparents, parents, children, aunts, etc.) lives under the same roof
- Sometimes we wonder why people make offerings to the gods every morning in the street
- Sometimes we wonder why people barricade themselves in their homes as soon as the sun goes down
- Sometimes we wonder why most of the 25-year-old women in the country are already married with several children
- Sometimes we wonder why people are so happy and smiling all the time

The best thing to do to gain an understanding is to ask why things are the way they are. The locals are usually happy that people are interested in them and will answer your questions with interest.

Making comparisons to develop critical thinking

When traveling, we develop a comparative view with our home country, its good points, its faults, its hang-ups, and its tapped and untapped potential.

For that matter, quite a few people think of leaving France (or whatever your home country may be) because of the problems they might have, but by visiting other countries, they realize that they're actually pretty fortunate.

That's one of the other powers of travel. You can realize very quickly how lucky you are.

Traveling alone also helps put our problems and misfortunes into perspective. For instance, the problems in our lives are often ridiculous compared to the challenges people in third world countries face every day. You have to see that to truly realize it.

By being alone during your trip, you will have the chance to soak up these details and differences more easily.

On a personal note

I think that each of my solo travels have enabled me to have a more open mind and a better understanding of the planet and the people who live on it.

My travels in countries like the Philippines and Indonesia have taught me humility and gratitude for the life I have as well as for my freedom.

I understand Anglo-Saxon culture better after spending several months in Canada and the United States. Despite my fascination with the energy and entrepreneurship in the United States, I definitely can't see myself living in a completely Americanized system.

By dint of experience, I think that one of the greatest skills I acquired is the ability to talk to any person without judgments or preconceptions.

The advantages of being very open-minded

This open-mindedness is beneficial on several levels.

You learn to trust other people and not to (unnecessarily) control everything. The more you travel, the more you realize that the vast majority of people don't wish you any harm. By making less assumptions about people, you can make concessions and have a trusting relationship.

By being more open-minded, you'll develop a different kind of critical eye. You'll understand the world better as well as the people around you and be able to argue your points of view with concrete examples.

You will be less resistant to new ideas and more tolerant because, with everything you've seen and done, you know that everything is possible in this world. Moreover, I noticed a certain humility among a majority of the travelers I've come across, along with a greater attentiveness.

Finally, I'd advise you to set out with an open perspective in order to absorb as much as you can during your trips. If you set out with a closed mind, it will be difficult to communicate, learn or evolve.

Chapter 13: Have Incredible Experiences

The eleventh benefit of solo travel is being able to enjoy your trip and all possible experiences to the max.

Having new adventures is a goal of any trip. When you're alone, this desire is intensified. You have to take maximum advantage of every moment and of the country you're in.

How do you move beyond the ordinary when you travel solo?

When traveling solo, the world is your oyster and you do what you want with it! You can say yes to anybody or anything if you want to.

By the way, that makes me think of the Jim Carrey film *Yes Man*.

Depressed, with both his professional life and love

life, which are at a standstill, Jim Carrey's character decides to say "Yes" right away to a personal development program. He then decides to seize every opportunity that's offered to him. If you saw the movie, you know that his work life improves considerably, he finds a girlfriend, and he has several adventures that spice up his life.

The parallel is similar here in your solo trip.

You shouldn't hesitate to say yes to what people suggest to you during your trip (within the limits of what's legal and moral, of course).

For example:

- Go out and have a drink with someone you just met
- Take a spontaneous excursion
- Join someone at a party
- Try a sport you've never done
- Accompany someone to a different destination

You have no idea how things might turn out, in a conventional way or in an epic way. To find out, you have to seize the opportunity and go for it.

Traveling solo, you have the chance to choose everything you want to do. You are 100% the master of your own destiny. It can be scary to follow someone into an adventure, but know that spontaneity often pays off when you're traveling.

On a personal note

I can't even count the number of times I've let myself be drawn into fantastic adventures or into half-assed plans. In both cases, you have a good story to tell afterwards!

I like going to parties where locals hang out and that are a little bit different. It's always more fun than big clubs that have no personality.

I remember something that happened in 2011 on the island of Palawan in the Philippines. After a day-long boat trip, a local woman told us that there was a big party in the neighboring village. Even though I was tired, I invited my French friend and an American to go there with me. We hired a tuk-tuk and driver, then took off for a 30-minute ride in the dark, not really knowing where we were going. When we got out in the middle of nowhere, we were astonished to see hundreds of people partying on a basketball court with music playing full-blast and local whiskey flowing freely. We were the only white people there and the star attractions of the evening. The end of the party is a bit foggy, but we had a great time all night. And, as far as local experiences go, it was unbeatable.

On a different note, I was able to visit the Kawah Ijen and Bromo volcanos in Indonesia all alone in December 2014. That was yet another crazy experience: getting up early, hiking through the night to watch the sunrise, and observing these natural wonders. You can't put a price on that!

Kayaking through a nature reserve in Canada, learning to ride a motorcycle in the Philippines, taking Highway 1 from Los Angeles to San Francisco, diving a wreck in Indonesia: they're all examples of when I said "yes" and seized the opportunity to have emotionally rich experiences.

What these experiences will change for you

You're going to realize that everything is possible.

When you're traveling, you can try everything and do things you may not have thought were possible. Like I say about challenges in Chapter 10, when you're traveling, you're a lot more likely to let loose and head for the unknown.

It's applicable to everyday life and not just to travel. Sometimes adventure is at the end of your street. I'm sure there are places near where you live that you haven't visited and activities that you haven't tried.

You can literally turn everything into an exciting adventure!

Experiencing the freedom to embrace any adventure that presents itself along the way is a powerful feeling, practically intoxicating. It's time for you to try it!

Chapter 14: Save Money

The twelfth and final benefit of solo travel is being able to save money.

That may seem strange. People usually say that traveling with a group allows you to share expenses, which is often true. But at the end of the day, when you travel solo, you have exclusive control over the decisions and can reduce your budget in several areas.

How can you spend less money?

1 — First of all, with your choice of destinations. Every country and every city has different prices. These destinations will have a big impact on your budget.

Depending on if you go to Indonesia or Japan, the overall cost can easily triple.

So choose your destinations carefully and find out the price of lodging, activities, food, and other things before you go.

These are examples of countries that are inexpensive, safe and interesting to visit: Indonesia, Thailand, Cambodia, India, Nicaragua, Ecuador, Bolivia, Hungary, and Romania.

The key here is not letting yourself get carried away by your friends to destinations that are expensive or beyond your budget. When you go alone, you make the decision based on *your* means.

To find out the cost of living in a country, there are two very informative websites:

- http://www.numbeo.com/
- http://www.expatistan.com/

2 — Next, you can decide when you'll leave, and that's an important point.

If you decide to travel during the peak season, everything will be more expensive, especially transportation and lodging. Travel during the off-season, or the shoulder season, and choose your travel dates with the cheapest flights possible using price comparison websites. My favorite is called Skyscanner.[8]

You can negotiate discounts for lodging and

---

[8] http://www.skyscanner.com/

activities more easily when you're there because there will be less tourists.

A quick Google search will give you information about the different seasons and the average number of visitors to your destinations.

3 — Finally, when you're alone, you have the option of sleeping where you want. You have no need to worry about the comfort level of your travel companions.

It's clear that for hotels and apartments of the Airbnb-type, being alone is often a disadvantage.

Opt for youth hostels – where the number of people doesn't change the price, or for small hotels or guest houses – where you can more easily negotiate the price (especially in the off-season). Or, of course, you can always stay in a private home thanks to Couchsurfing. When you are alone, your chances of being accepted by a host on Couchsurfing are greater. You'll almost never have problems.

On a personal note

As for me, I avoid the high seasons as much as possible or else I plan things out well in advance. However, I really don't like it when a place is full of tourists!

When I visit a country where the cost of living is

high, in order to pay less, I organize things by planning to cook for myself. I prefer hostels or using Couchsurfing. For example, I spent two weeks in California in January 2015 and I didn't spend a single night in a hotel. Instead, I stayed with friends and Couchsurfers.

In any case, I prefer visiting countries that have a low cost of living, where I don't spend much money. I'm currently in Colombia, where prices are generally three times cheaper than in France!

You can enjoy the extra money

I think you can really save money by traveling solo, by making decisions that suit you and your personal budget.

For example, you can allocate a bigger budget to on-site activities in order to have incredible experiences. There can be activities with considerable price tags, like scuba diving, some extreme sports, and multi-day treks.

Everything depends on your priorities.

Chapter 15: Jérémy's Story

We're almost to the end of the book, so it's time to treat you to the second exclusive interview from another traveler who decided to go it alone.

It's Jérémy Marie, who traveled around the world hitchhiking for five years. He's a traveler I really admire. He did what few people could do, including myself, and I'm thrilled that he agreed to be in the book.

You can find more of his stories on his blog (in French): http://tour-du-monde-autostop.fr/

1 — When did you set out alone and for how long?

I set out at the time of my life between the end of my studies and the beginning of my working life. In my case, that was at the age of 23. It was October 8, 2007.

I came back five years, five months, and five days

later, on March 12, 2013. I was exactly 29 years old that day.

2 — What continents/countries have you visited?

This trip around the world allowed me to experience a total of 71 countries and territories. My plan was to travel only by hitchhiking, so I traveled 180,700 kilometers (112,282 miles), with the help of 1,752 different vehicles and just as many generous drivers.

The itinerary first took me from Caen toward Istanbul. I crossed Western Europe and the Balkans to get there. Next, I headed for the Middle East and I was able to visit Syria before the revolutions of the Arab Spring. Next, my route took me from Cairo to Cape Town, crossing the entire African continent from the north to the south along its eastern coast, wandering through Ethiopia, Malawi, and Sudan. From Cape Town, I crossed the ocean by boat hitchhiking toward Central America and its unmissable commercial hub, Panama. I then spent a year roaming around North America, all the way to Fairbanks, Alaska. Then, I spent another year going around South America, as far as its southernmost point Ushuaia, and ended up in Cartagena, Colombia.

In Colombia, I found a job as a crewmember on a sailboat which allowed me to spend four months floating in the direction of Auckland, New Zealand, with the inevitable idyllic stops in the Galapagos, French Polynesia, and Tonga.

Then, I went from New Zealand to Australia by hitching a ride on a container ship, from Australia to Indonesia with airplane-hitchhiking, before heading through Southeast Asia toward the Chinese Middle Kingdom. From China, I crossed all of Central Asia and its "Stan" countries and experienced Persian culture in Iran before returning to Turkey and crossing Europe again in the other direction to finally reach my point of departure in Caen (in Normandy) where I was greeted by the unexpected snowfall in the month of March 2013.

3 — Why did you decide to travel solo?

At that point in my life, I wanted to develop an understanding of the world around me, particularly from the point of view of its population. Traveling around the world was certainly the best way to put together these points of view, especially since the mode of transportation I wanted to use would necessarily bring me into close contact with the populations of the countries I was crossing.

Traveling alone by hitchhiking constantly leads you to open up to the other person because you're dependent on him to get to the next leg. The clear advantage of traveling alone in this case is that I was a lot more open to meeting people, which allowed me to learn more about the cultures of the people I encountered.

4 — What's your best memory of the trip?

Let's say that my best travel memory influenced my life today. When I was on the island of Bali, I met a young Indonesian woman who is now my wife.

I should say that at the end of half a decade spent alone on the road, I was starting to want new things. I had come out of my shell by meeting other people, but as my plan constantly pushed me to cut these social interactions short to get to the next destination, I naturally developed the desire to form a long-term relationship, to have a family.

To back this up, I'd like to share a Melanesian myth from the Vanuatu archipelago that I recently came across which, I think, perfectly illustrates this desire:

Every man is torn between two needs: the need of the Canoe, in other words, travel, and the need of the Tree, which is putting down roots, identity. Men drift constantly between these two needs, sometimes giving in to one, sometimes to the other. Until the day when they realize it's with the Tree that one makes the Canoe.

-Melanesian myth from the Vanuatu archipelago

5 — What was your worst experience?

Oddly enough, my worst experience didn't happen with my favorite mode of transportation, which is hitchhiking. Even though a lot of people I met thought that it was a dangerous way to get around, I never experienced any violence from my temporary drivers, although it's true that I did meet some very unusual people.

No, the worst violence, and therefore the worst experience I fell victim to, happened in the center of Caracas in Venezuela. I was relieved of my few valuable objects, held up at gunpoint, by the city police. And oddly enough, for that, there was no need to stick my thumb out on the side of the road.

6 — Can you tell us a story that illustrates what "solo travel" means to you?

Solo travel offers a wide range of possibilities. With a little bit of creativity, you're often limited only by your desire, no matter what the destination. In my case, I think my crossing the Pacific by sailboat-hitchhiking demonstrates the unfathomable possibilities of "solo travel" really well.

In March 2011, I was scouring the marinas and yacht clubs of Cartagena de Indias, Colombia in order to find transportation that would take me to the other side of the

Pacific to Australia. Based on my experience with sailboat-hitchhiking between South Africa and Panama, I knew that the best way was to go to each captain on each boat and to offer my services as "cook/night watchman/potato peeler."

After a few days, I was accepted aboard the sailboat *Khamsin* which was slated to sail to Auckland, New Zealand. There's no question that being alone made the difference at this time, because the sailboat was already full. The essential condition for my acceptance on board was that my bed would be in the boat's mess, namely in the public area of the craft. My high tolerance for noise when falling asleep and my low requirements for comfort meant that at that moment, I became the seventh and final crewman on the *Khamsin* for that Pacific crossing. Being alone at that moment was definitely an advantage. I can only imagine that if I had headed to the pier with a travel partner my potential of joining a crew wouldn't even have been considered. It's possible that I'd still be in Colombia wandering through departure points of outbound vessels.

7 — What was your assessment of that first solo trip?

I was flourishing when I returned.

One of the main reasons is that one of my main goals in life is to find a meaning in my existence, and therefore to be interested in and to learn about every subject. I think that this long trip kept me busy full-time in these areas and have the feeling to at least having taken some action in this endeavor.

Traveling around the world alone implies coming face-to-face with new cultures, learning about new ways to live and to think. That really broadened the constraints of the Western mentality I felt stuck in before I left. By approaching and sharing with different civilizations, I at least have the possibility of believing that different ways of life are possible if I ever felt like changing the way I live.

8 — In your opinion, why should everyone try traveling solo?

Traveling solo is a personal process, and as a result, the lessons learned allow you to know yourself a little better. In order to lead a life that's happy and meaningful, I think it's necessary to identify not only your passions, but also the things that don't interest you. Traveling solo allows you to more easily access those situations in which you're forced to make personal decisions and to think about them. Traveling alone, in just a few words, is a true learning experience about yourself and about life in general.

9 — With your experience, what advice would you give to "Pre-Travel Jérémy"?

I think that the greatest difficulties before a long-term trip are related to the decision to leave.

Uncertainties grow when faced with the unknown and fear comes out. The advice that I'd give to "Pre-Travel Jérémy," and also to anyone else who wants to have a go, would be to fight that fear and not to hesitate to hit the road, because behind that fear hides a mass of wonderful meetings and unique learning experiences.

Thank you, Jérémy, for sharing your story.

Conclusion

Traveling solo is scary.

Traveling alone isn't easy.

However, I hope you've seen that the rewards and benefits of this kind of trip are huge. You will no longer be the same person after a solo trip. You will be transformed.

You will have more self-confidence, be more independent, resourceful, sociable, adventurous, and open-minded.

It's impossible to list everything, but I think you can appreciate all of the benefits of solo travel after reading this book.

Stop paying attention to what people say. Stop paying attention to the traditional travel formula suggested by the media and society.

Live the life you want to live, without waiting for other people.

Fellow travelers or soon-to-be travelers, go towards the unknown and set out solo to find the world!

You won't regret it, I promise.

Michael's Final Note

Thank you so much for buying the first volume of the "Solo Travel Guide."

I am very proud to finally have this book available in English. French, unfortunately, is not spoken by many people, therefore, I wasn't able to share my work with everyone, which was frustrating for me. As I travel, I make so many friends all over the world, so I HAD to write the book in English as well.

I hope you liked it. And, if you did, I would be super grateful if you'd give me a review on Amazon. Or, if you prefer, you can write me an email; I'd love to connect with you.

Thank you to everyone one of you that helped me in any way with the book.

To stay in touch:

- Email: michael@traverserlafrontiere.com
- Website: http://traverserlafrontiere.com/en/

Good travels to you all.

- Michael

Made in the USA
Middletown, DE
20 July 2017